A Primer
for the

CATHOLIC
CHOIR
MEMBER

Lawrence J. Johnson

Pastoral Press
Portland, Oregon

ISBN 1-56929-064-4

© 1996 Pastoral Press
A Division of OCP
5536 N.E. Hassalo
Portland, OR 97213
Phone: 800-LITURGY (548-8749)
Email: liturgy@ocp.org
Web site: www.pastoralpress.com
Web site: www.ocp.org

CONTENTS

A Word of Introduction

One of the most important things a Christian people do is to gather on the Lord's Day so that its members may sit at the table of God's word and at the table of the Lord's eucharist. Listening to the stories of one's spiritual forebears (stories in which we also play a part) and sharing in the Lord's body and blood allow us not only to grow as Christians, but also to reveal in ritual fashion what it means to be a community forming the very Body of Christ in the world today.

This gathering of Christians—often called the *assembly*—requires the special talents of many people: for example, that of a presider who has acquired the skills of leading a people at prayer; the skills of a reader or of readers who not merely read a printed text but who have the ability to energize minds and hearts through the ageless power and beauty of God's written word.

Among the numerous services or ministries that make the assembly possible is that of the choir. A choir, whether its members be few or numerous, whether its musical talents be abundant or modest, exists for one purpose. Unlike the school, community, or symphony chorus which is a performance organization, the liturgical choir serves the people who have come together for prayer. More specifically, the choir serves this people's *sung* prayer.

The choir does so in two principal ways. It participates in the assembly's song, either directly (singing with and as part of the people) or indirectly, as it were, by embellishing and enhancing this song in various ways (e.g., descants, harmony, alteration). There are also moments when the choir can sing by itself, helping to create an atmosphere within which, through the prompting of the Holy Spirit, true prayer can happen. To be sure, the choir serves the demanding art of music, but it does so as a servant of the people, the faithful, the baptized who have responded to God's invitation to render communal praise.

The members of a choir form one of the numerous communities that make up the contemporary parish. As a community, these members rely upon one another for psychological and musical support. Singing together, and especially rehearsing, offer occasions for group patience, discipline, and solidarity. Singing together allows us to enjoy one another's company and to experience the love and friendship of other pilgrims who join us on our journey with Jesus through life.

To journey, whether musically or spiritually, means to move ahead, to progress, to search for that tomorrow when everything, in some way, will be better. Some of us may be novice choristers, just beginning to learn about notes, repertory, choral techniques, and the like. Others among us may be old hands, veterans who have weathered in good spirits changes in the liturgy, new pastors, and even new choir directors. Yet each of us is called to grow, to improve our musical knowledge and our understanding of worship. It was for such a purpose that this booklet was written.

1

STAFF AND CLEF

The Staff. Musical notes are written upon a series of horizontal equally distant lines, called a staff.

The Clef Sign. This is a symbol placed at the beginning of a staff to indicate a specific pitch on that staff. Singers ordinarily encounter two different clef signs.

A. The G or treble clef sign (sopranos, altos, and sometimes tenors).

B. The F or bass clef sign (basses and sometimes tenors).

Notes on the Staff. Each note upon the staff has a letter name.

C D E F G A B C D E F G A B C

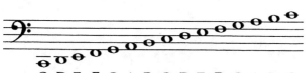

C D E F G A B C D E F G A B C

NOTES AND RESTS

Types of Notes. The following types of notes are common in choral music.

Whole note   𝅝

Half note   𝅗𝅥

Quarter note   ♩

Eighth note   ♪

Sixteenth note   𝅘𝅥𝅯

Relative Value of Notes.

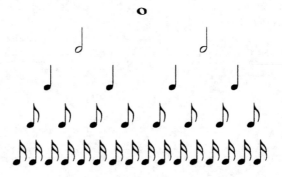

Types of Rests. Just as each note is indicated by a symbol, so each period of silence within the music is indicated by a symbol.

Whole note rest

Half note rest

Quarter note rest

Eighth note rest

Sixteenth note rest

The Dot. A dot placed after a note or rest indicates that the length of the note or rest is augmented by one half. Some examples:

TIME VALUES

The **time value** (often called the meter) of a musical piece is indicated by a symbol placed toward the beginning of the staff.

The **top part** of the symbol indicates the number of beats in a measure.

The **bottom part** of the symbol indicates the type of note receiving a beat.

Examples:

Symbol	Number of beats in the measure	Type of note or its equivalent
3/4	3	♩
3/8	3	♪
4/4	4	♩
2/2	2	𝅗𝅥

Some composers use the symbol **C** for 4/4 and **₵** for 2/2.

4

STEPS, SCALES, AND KEYS

Step. The pitch relationship between any two contiguous notes or tones is called a half-step. For example, the distance between C and the C# immediately above it is a half-step. The distance between C and D is two half-steps or a whole step.

Scale. Musical notes are arranged into various series or patterns (usually comprising 8 notes). They differ according to where the whole steps or half-steps between the notes are placed. This pattern is called a scale.

Major Scale. A scale or pattern having a whole step between each note except for half-steps between the 3rd and 4th notes and between the 7th note and the octave.

Minor Scale. Each major scale has a related "minor" scale which begins 3 half-steps lower than the 1st note of the related major scale.

Key Signature. This indicates the note on which a particular scale (whether the major or minor) begins.

Steps, Scales, and Keys

Examples

Key Signature	*Treble*	*Bass*
C Major or a minor		
G Major or e minor		
D Major or b minor		
A Major or f♯ minor		
E Major or c♯ minor		
F Major or d minor		
B-flat Major or minor		
E-flat Major or c minor		
A-flat Major or f minor		

5

SINGING IN ENGLISH

Any number of books and manuals have been written on singing in English. What follows summarizes a few major areas of this technique.

Vowels

1. The basic building block of all singing (and thus of singing in English) is the **vowel**.

2. In English there are five primary vowel sounds: *ooh* (*who*); *oh* (*woe*); *ah* (*lah*); *ay* (*way*); *ee* (*we*).

3. There are also numerous variations of these vowel sounds, e.g., *aw* (*laud*); *eh* (*let*), etc.

4. Remember, sing to the end of the vowel sound and sustain its tone quality.

5. Do not change the quality of the vowel as you ascend to higher notes.

Diphthongs

6. The English language also contains what are called **diphthongs**; a diphthong is a sound

formed by two consecutive vowels in one syllable.

7. Each component of a diphthong is sounded distinctly, e.g., *day (day-ee)*; *high (hah-ee)*; *new (nee-oo)*, etc. The first vowel sound, however, is generally given prominence.

Consonants

8. **Consonants** may be considered as the gates through which we pass from one vowel sound to the next.

9. Consonants are either voiced or unvoiced (resonant or non-resonant).

10. A voiced consonant requires a vocalized sound, whereas a voiceless consonant requires a blowing of air; there are often pairs of consonants where there is the same position of the speech organs for each . . . and thus it is important that the singer take special care that *"on the vine"* not be sung as *"on the fine."*

Voiceless	Voiced	
t	*d*	
f	*v*	
p	*b*	
s	*z*	etc.

Connecting/Dividing Syllables within the Word

11. The way a word is divided on the printed page may not necessarily be the way your director will ask you to divide the word. For example:

Printed	Sung
seat-ed	*sea-ted*
dif-fer-ence	*di-ffe-rence*
bless-ed	*ble-sed*
mas-ter	*ma-ster*

12. Generally speaking, consonants are carried forward so that they begin the next syllable.

Connecting/Separating Words

13. The connection and non-connection between words, especially in legato singing, is very important.

    * If the first word ends in a consonant, this consonant is quite often carried over to the second word: e.g., *kiss me* (*ki-sme*); *his own* (*hi-zown*).

    * When the same consonants occur at the end of one word and at the beginning of the second word, generally omit one of the conso-

11

nants: e.g., *send down* (*sen-down*).

* When the first word ends in the same vowel sound that begins the second word, separate the two words: e.g., *three / eagles* (and not *threeeagles*).

* Always separate words if a mistake in hearing would occur by linking them together: e.g., *deaf / ears* (not *dea-fears*).

* Words may be separated to give them special effect: e.g., *his / silent journey*.

What Not to Stress

14. Do not stress prepositions (*of, at, to*), conjunctions (*and*), or articles (*the, a, an*).

15. Do not emphasize consonants like *s, z, sh, ch,* and the soft *c.* Doing so results in a very unmusical effect. Generally these consonants are linked to the following syllable or word: e.g., *ma-ster.*

A Consonant with Special Rules

16. The consonant *r* has some special rules.

* It is never sung before another consonant: e.g., *summer day* is sung *summe' day*

* It is not sung before a pause.

* It is always sung before a vowel.

Look Ahead!

17. Always sing to the end of the word, to the end of the phrase. Look ahead!

Beginnings and Endings

18. A slight unobtrusive *h* sound helps facilitate attacks that begin with a vowel: e.g., (h) *O bone Jesu.*

19. Singers need to pay special attention to releases concluding with consonants like *s, z, sh, ch* to avoid the "snake" effect: e.g., *fears* sung as *fearssssss.* The same is true for the final d and t.

Overcoming Inertia

20. We cannot afford to "sing as we speak." Doing so results in *"Whajuheet?"* for *"What did you eat?"* Singing requires that we overcome the natural inertia found in daily speech.

LATIN PRONUNCIATION

Latin pronunciation is less complex than English pronunciation. There are not as many rules and fewer exceptions to these rules. What follows is a summary of the Roman or liturgical method of pronouncing Latin.

Vowels

Letter	English Word	Latin Word
a	*father*	*pater*
e, ae, oe	*red*	*etiam*
i, y	*feet*	*gloria*
o	*foe*	*Deo*
u	*tune*	*cum*

* When two or more vowels come together, each vowel must be sounded: e.g., *filius* (*fee-lee-oos*).

* The exception is, as noted above, *ae* and *oe* have one sound, the sound of *e*: e.g. *caelum* (*che-loom*).

* The vowels *ou, ai, au, eu,* and *ay,* although forming one syllable, are sounded individually: e.g. *lauda* (*la-uda*).

* The vowel *u* preceded by *q* or *ng* and followed by another vowel in words like *qui* and *sanguis* is

uttered as one syllable with the vowel that follows: e.g., *qui, quae, quod, sanguis* (*kwee*, etc.)

* And yet the word *cui* is generally sounded with two syllables: e.g. *koo-ee*.

Consonants

b pronounced as in English

c 1) pronounced *ch* (as in *church*) before *i, e, ae, oe, y*: e.g., *caeli* (*che-lee*)
2) *cc* before those same vowels is pronounced *t-ch*: e.g., *ecce* (*et-che*)
3) at all other times *c* is pronounced as *k*: e.g., *cum* (*koom*)
4) *ch* is always pronounced as *k*: e.g., *chorus* (*ko-roos*)

d pronounced as in English

f pronounced as in English

g 1) always soft (as in *general*) before *e, i, ae, oe, y*: e.g., *genitor*
2) *gn* is pronounced *ny*: e.g., *magnam* (*mah-nyam*)
3) before all other vowels the *g* is hard, as in *government*

15

Latin Pronunciation

h 1) silent
   2) except for *mihi* and *nihil* (*mee-hee, nee-heel*)

j often written as *i* and pronounced as *y* forming one sound with the following vowel: e.g., *jam* (*yam*)

k pronounced as in English

l pronounced as in English

m pronounced as in English

n pronounced as in English

p pronounced as in English

q pronounced as in English

r rolled slightly with the tongue

s 1) hard (as in *sea*)
   2) slightly softened when it occurs between two vowels: e.g., *misericordia*
   3) *sc* before *e, i, ae, oe, y*, is pronounced like the English *sh* (as in *shed*): e.g., *suscepi* (*su-she-pee*)

t 1) pronounced as in English: e.g., *totus*
   2) *ti* appearing before a vowel and following any

letter (except *s, x, t*) is pronounced *t-see*: e.g., *gratia* (*grat-see-a*)

th pronounced as *t*: e.g., *catholicam* (*ka-to-lee-kam*)

v pronounced as in English

x 1) like the English *ks*: e.g., *exercitus* (*eks-er-chee-tus*)
   2) *xc* before *e, ae, oe, i, y* is pronounced as *k-sh*: e.g., *excelsis* (*ek-shel-sees*)
   3) before other vowels *xc* has the hard sounds of the letters composing it: e.g., *excussorum* (*eks-coos-so-rum*)

z (rare in liturgical Latin) pronounced *dz*: e.g., *zona* (*dzo-na*)

* Double consonants: clearly sound each consonant: e.g., *bello* (*bel-lo*).

7

REHEARSALS; THE LITURGY

1. Never forget that the goal of your choir's singing is to assist and enhance the communal prayer of the people who gather for worship, namely, the assembly.

2. Perhaps your parish has several choirs, each focusing upon a particular type of repertoire. Rejoice! These groups do not compete against one another but rather share in the same ministry or service to the people.

3. Take an active role in recruiting new members for your choir. Sharing your good choral experiences with a friend and asking him or her to join the group can result in a new recruit (in most choirs this will be a double blessing if the friend is a tenor).

4. Make new members of the choir feel welcome; help them to become acquainted with the veteran members (perhaps each new member should be given a sponsor).

5. If, for one reason or another, you cannot be present for a rehearsal or a liturgical celebra-

tion, be sure to phone your choir director beforehand so that he or she can, if necessary, make any adjustments.

6. Remember that everyone benefits when each choir member arrives on time for rehearsals and the liturgy. It's called punctuality.

7. Good posture is essential to good tone production.

8. When standing, be sure your spine is straight (do not hump over); keep your head erect; do not pull back your shoulders; be sure your feet are slightly apart with one foot slightly in front of the other.

9. When sitting, do not slouch; sit up straight; do not lean all the way back in the chair; place both feet on the floor (do not cross your legs);

10. Hold your music at such a height so that you can see both music and conductor at the same time.

11. We all must breathe to live; and singers must breathe to sing. Don't wait till your lungs are ready to burst; catch quick staggered breaths along the way.

Rehearsals; The Liturgy

12. Take a deep breath (preferably through the nose) immediately before you begin to sing; mentally prepare yourself for this attack.

13. Good musical starts and good endings do not a good choir make, but they sure can help.

14. As you sing, listen to others around you. You are part of a group.

15. Cough drops, chewing gum, and M&Ms do not help facilitate good choral tone.

16. Plan ahead for page-turns during your singing. Slightly anticipate the action; don't wait till the very last minute.

17. Be patient while the director is rehearsing other sections of the choral group; your turn will eventually come.

18. If you or your vocal section has trouble with an interval or phrase, don't fake it. Ask your director for assistance.

19. When not singing during the liturgy, center your attention upon the focal point of the liturgical action, e.g., upon the reader during

the reading, upon the homilist during the homily, etc.

20. All of us need encouragement—including your choral director.

21. Life requires that we constantly grow; we can do no less as choral singers in our skills, repertory, and general musical/liturgical knowledge.

"At times the choir, within the congregation of the faithful and as part of it, will assume the role of leadership, while at other times it will retain its own distinctive ministry. This means that the choir will lead the people in sung prayer, by alternating or reinforcing the sacred song of the congregation, or by enhancing it with the addition of a musical elaboration. At other times in the course of liturgical celebration the choir alone will sing works whose musical demands enlist and challenge its competence." Bishops' Committee on the Liturgy, *Music in Catholic Worship* (1972), no. 36.

8

MUSICAL GLOSSARY

A cappella. Unaccompanied.

Accelerando (accel.). Increase the speed.

Accent. Stressing one tone over others.

Accidentals. Musical symbols placed at the left side of the head of a note to raise, lower, or return to normal the pitch of a note, e.g., sharps, flats, etc.

Adagio. Slowly.

Allegro. Lively.

Alto. The part above the tenor.

Andante. A moderate tempo; somewhat slowly.

Animato. Animated; with spirit.

Appasionato. Intensely.

Assai. Very; extremely; much.

Attack. The way in which the beginning of a musical phrase is sung or played.

Balance. The distribution of tonal weight between two or more sections of a choir or other musical group.

Bar-Line. A vertical line drawn through one or more staves of music to indicate the measures of a composition; in the U.S. the word **bar** designates a measure.

Bass. The lowest voice part.

Beat. The unit of measurement indicated by the motion of the conductor's stick or arms.

Blend. The quality of tone within a particular voice section and between various voice sections.

Cadence. A concluding phrase of a musical piece or of a section within that piece; the term is often applied to the harmony used in that phrase.

Canon. A polyphonic musical composition in which one part is imitated by one or more other parts, though not on the same pitch.

Capo. The beginning; the head.

Chant. A general designation for music that is sung in unison, that is unaccompanied, and in free rhythm, e.g., Gregorian Chant.

Chorale. A hymn tune, usually of the Protestant Church.

Chord. The simultaneous sounding of three or more notes.

Chromatic alteration. The raising or lowering of a note by means of an accidental.

Clef. From the Latin *clavis* ("key"), a sign placed at the beginning of a staff to indicate a specific pitch, e.g., the G Clef or the F Clef.

Coda. A passage at the conclusion of a musical piece or movement.

Common time. Having two beats in a bar or any multiplication of two beats.

Crescendo (cresc.) A gradual increase in power.

Da Capo (D.C.). From the beginning.

Decrescendo. (decr.) Gradually diminishing the power.

Descant. An independent and often somewhat

elaborate melody sung over another melody

Diatonic. A natural scale composed of five whole tones and two semitones and having no chromatic tones, e.g. the scale of C as played on the white notes of the keyboard.

Diminuendo (dim.). See **Decrescendo**.

Dot. Used after a note to indicate that its time value is increased by one-half.

Double Bar. Two vertical lines drawn through the staff at the end of a section, movement, or piece.

Dynamics. The degrees of loudness and softness in a composition; the signs by which these are indicated.

Fermata. A pause, indicated by the sign ⌒.

Flag. The symbol placed on the right side of the stem of a note which halves its value.

Flat. A sign indicating that the pitch of a note is lowered by a half-step.

Forte (f). Loud; strong.

Fortissimo (ff). Very loud.

Grave. Very slow and solemn.

Harmony. A generic term designating the composition and progression of chords.

Inner Parts. The alto and tenor voice parts.

Interval. The distance in pitch between any two notes.

Intonation. Singing or playing in tune; the opening notes of a Gregorian melody.

Key. A scale, with the key (or keynote) being the first note of that scale.

Largo. Slowly, broadly.

Larynx. That organ by which we produce vocal sounds; it is located at the top of the wind pipe.

Ledger Lines. Short lines above or below the staff used to indicated notes that are too high or too low to be indicated on the staff.

Legato. Smoothly.

Lento. Slowly.

Maestoso. Majestically; stately.

Major, Minor. Adjectives designating: (1) certain types of intervals (e.g., a major second, a minor third); a type of scale (e.g., a minor scale); a key based upon a major or minor scale (e.g., the key of c-minor).

Measure. The space between two bar lines.

Melismatic. Using many notes for one syllable of the text.

Melody. An organized pattern of three or more notes played or sung in succession.

Meter. The basic and unaltered scheme of note values and accents found throughout a composition or a section thereof.

Mode. An arrangement of tones forming the tonal substance of a composition.

Moderato. Moderately.

Modulation. Moving from one key to another within a composition.

Molto. Much; extremely.

Monody. Music for a single voice or a unison group with only one note being heard at a time,

Musical Glossary

e.g., Gregorian Chant.

Monophony. See **Monody**.

Natural. A sign indicating that after a sharp or a flat the original tone is restored.

Neume. The name for a note or a group of notes in Gregorian Chant.

Notation. The recording of music in writing by means of various signs and symbols.

Octave. An interval consisting of eight diatonic tones; the eighth tone of such an interval.

Octavo. Refers to the size of paper upon which a musical composition is printed, namely, paper cut eight from a sheet.

Ostinato. A repeated melodic pattern (usually in the bass) over which the other parts change.

Part Music. Harmonized music.

Passage. A term that refers to a short section of a composition.

Phrase. A unit of a melody, often two to eight measures in length.

Piano. Softly.

Pitch. The relative highness or lowness of a tone.

Piu. More.

Poco. Little.

Polyphony. A style of music in which there is a combination of two or more melodies rather than one main melody supported by various chords.

Presto. Very quickly.

Rallentando. Gradually decreasing the tempo.

Refrain. Recurring lines of a poem and usually set

to the same music, e.g., a chorus.

Release. The way in which the very end of a musical phrase is performed.

Repeat. A sign indicating that the whole composition or a section thereof is to be repeated.

Rest. A symbol used to indicate a period of silence.

Rhythm. The principle of alternating tension and relaxation in the temporal duration of tones.

Ritardando (rit.). Gradually becoming slower

Round. A type of canon in which each part is continuously repeated.

Scale. A series of tones arranged in an ascending or descending pattern.

Sharp. The sign placed after a note that raises the note's pitch one-half tone.

Sight-Reading. Performing music without previous preparation.

Signature. A sign placed at the beginning of a composition to indicate the key or the meter.

Slur. A curved line placed over or under a group of notes indicating that the notes are to be played legato or sung in one breath.

Solfeggio. Vocal exercises using the syllables do, re, mi, etc.

Soprano. The highest voice.

Space. The interval between two lines in a staff.

Staff. A series of horizontal equally distant lines upon or between which the notes are written.

Stanza. A section of a poem having a specific

Musical Glossary

pattern of meter and rhyme.

Step. The interval between two contiguous degrees of a scale.

Syncopation. The deliberate upsetting of rhythm, meter, or accent.

Tablature. A general name applied to the whole body of signs and characters used in writing music.

Tempo. The speed at which a musical composition moves.

Tenor. The part above the lowest male voice.

Tessitura. The range of a melody or voice part.

Tie. A curved line joining two notes of the same pitch.

Time. A term customarily applied to the number of beats in each meassure and the value given to each beat, e.g., 3/4 time as indicating that there are three quarter notes in each measure.

Tone. A musical note; the interval of a major second, e.g., between C and D; the quality of a sound; a melodic formula for singing the psalms.

Transpose. To perform a piece in another key.

Tremolo. In singing, a slight variation in pitch.

Tune. A melody, often an easily remembered melody.

Tune, In. Singing or playing on the correct musical pitch.

Un poco. A little.

Unequal Voices. Male and female voices in one choir.

Unison. Two or more notes of the same pitch.
Vibrato. See **Tremolo**.
Vivace. Very quickly.
Vocalization. Singing a melody on one vowel.

"A well-trained choir adds beauty and solemnity to the liturgy and also assists and encourages the singing of the congregation. The Second Vatican Council, speaking of the choir, stated emphatically that 'the whole body of the faithful may be able to contribute that active participation which is rightly theirs.'"
Bishops' Committee on the Liturgy, *Music in Catholic Worship* (1972), no. 36.

9

LITURGICAL GLOSSARY

Acclamation. A liturgical/musical form that might be compared to a shout (of joy) by a group of people, an enthusiastic outburst of praise.

Agnus Dei. See **Lamb of God**.

Alleluia. From the Hebrew *hallelu-jah* ("praise the Lord"), the word "Alleluia" is an expression of joy and peace.

Amen. From the Hebrew for "so be it," a word used in Christian liturgy as a sign that the people consent to a prayer.

Anaphora (from the Greek for "offering"). The customary name for the eucharistic prayer in the eastern churches.

Anthem. (From the Old English *antefn*, a word derived from the Greek "antiphona", a choral composition with English words (from Scripture, religious poetry) and often accompanied by organ.

Antiphon. A composition or refrain sung in connection with a psalm or canticle.

Antiphonal Psalmody. Singing the verses of a psalm by alternating groups of singers.

Assembly. The people who gather for worship.

Canticle. A song-like text found in the Scriptures and yet not taken from the Book of Psalms.

Cantor. From the Latin *cantare* (to sing), this noun

has been applied to the person (1) who intones or begins certain chants; (2) who sings the verses of the psalm; (3) who leads the singing of the people.

Choir. A group of church singers or a group that sings "religious" music.

Chorale. A term designating the text and melody of German hymns, especially those of the Protestant Reformation.

Chorister. In general, any person who sings in a choir, but often used of a boy choir member.

Communion Song. The psalm, hymn, or other text sung during the distribution of the eucharist.

Compline. From the Latin *completorium* ("ending"), this is the former name for the prayer that concluded the divine office; today it is simply called "night prayer."

Creed. See **Profession of Faith**.

Doxology. From the Greek *doxa*(glory) and *logos* (word), a text of praise, usually of the Trinity.

Entrance Song. The vocal music (hymnody, psalmody), sung by the people, that actually begins the Mass.

Eucharistic Prayer (Latin, *prex eucharistica*). The central and consecratory prayer of the Mass whereby priest and people bless, praise, and give thanks to God; it begins with the dialog introducing the preface and concludes with the Great Amen.

General Intercessions. The litanic prayer concluding the liturgy of the word. Also known as the prayer of the faithful, the universal prayer, and (in England) the bidding prayer.

Glory to God. (Latin title: *Gloria in excelsis*). An ancient Christian hymn which begins with the song of the angels at Bethlehem.

Gospel Book. A special type of lectionary, one containing only the gospel passages; it is also called an evangelistary.

Great Amen. The concluding Amen of the eucharistic prayer whereby the assembly sings or speaks its affirmation to the prayer.

Hosanna. A Hebrew shout of praise to God.

Hymn. A musical setting of a poetical text which ordinarily gives praise to God.

Kyrie eleison (Greek for "Lord, have mercy"). Originally the people's response to a litany that was a forerunner of our general intercessions. Today it occurs during the introductory rites either as a separate litany or as part of the penitential rite.

Lamb of God. The series of invocations sung during the breaking of the bread. These invocations (in Latin the *Agnus Dei*) were introduced into the Roman Mass by Pope Sergius I (d. 701).

Lectionary. A volume containing the scriptural readings for Mass and the responsorial psalms.

Litany. From the Greek *litanos* (meaning "entreaty"), a litany is a series of petitions sung or recited by a leader; after each of these the people answer with a fixed response.

Liturgy. Literally from the Greek, "the work of the

people," a term used today to designate the common ritual prayer of the assembled Christian people.

Liturgy of the Eucharist. The second of the two major sections of the Mass; it consists of the rites of preparation, the eucharistic prayer, and the communion rite; the liturgy of the eucharist concludes with the prayer after communion.

Liturgy of the Hours. Also known as the "divine office" or "the canonical hours." The official prayer of the church by which the hours of the day are sanctified. Its sections (often called "hours") are linked to the various times of the day.

Liturgy of the Word. The first of the two major sections of the Mass; beginning after the introductory rites, it consists of scriptural readings, chants, homily, intercessions (and at times the profession of faith).

Mass. From the Latin *missa* ("being sent"), this is a traditional term for the celebration of the liturgy of the word and that of the eucharist.

Motet. From the French *mot* ("word"), a choral composition with a religious (usually Latin) text and originally unaccompanied.

Ordinary of the Mass. An expression, used more and more infrequently today, designating texts generally common to all Masses, e.g., the Lord's Prayer, the Lamb of God.

Ordinary Time. A term designating that section of the liturgical year having no distinctive emphasis

Liturgical Glossary

(as we find in Advent or Lent). Ordinary Time begins on the Monday after the Sunday following January 6 and continues till the Tuesday before Ash Wednesday; the season resumes on the Monday after Pentecost Sunday and continues till the beginning of Advent.

Pericope. A passage from the Scriptures that is assigned to be read at a particular liturgy.

Plainsong. A designation for Gregorian Chant and other types of unison, unaccompanied liturgical music. Also called *plainchant.*

Preface. The opening section of the eucharistic prayer; it begins with the dialogue "The Lord be with you" and concludes with a mention of the angels.

Preparation Rite. The first part of the liturgy of the eucharist during which the altar, gifts, and people are prepared for the eucharistic prayer. This rite was formerly called the "offertory."

Processional. A procession that enters a church building, or any music that accompanies this procession

Profession of Faith. At Mass the Nicene Creed (a summary of the beliefs of the Fathers at the Councils of Nicaea [325] and of Constantinope [381]). This form of the creed came into the west from the east by way of Spain and Gaul; it became part of the Roman Mass only in the eleventh century.

Psalter. A book containing the psalms, whether text only or text together with music.

Psalm. A poem found in the Old Testament's Book of Psalms.

Psalm Tones. Melodic formulas used for chanting the psalms.

Psalmody. The art of singing the psalms.

Psalms, Metrical. Vernacular and metered translations of the psalms allowing them to be sung to hymn tunes.

Recessional. The action whereby the ministers depart from the altar after a liturgical service; the hymn or other music sung or played to accompany this action.

Rite. A term having several meanings: (a) the totality of actions and words used during a particular liturgical function (e.g., the rite of baptism); (b) individual elements in a totality (e.g., the rite of pouring water); (c) the liturgical tradition, practices, and spiritualities of particular churches (e.g., the Roman rite, the Byzantine rite, etc.)

Responsorial Psalm. The psalm following the first reading; it is not so much a "response" to the Scripture that has been read but a proclamation in song of God's goodness, fidelity, and love.

Responsorial Psalmody. The practice whereby a soloist (or even a choir) sings the verses of a psalm, and the whole assembly responds by singing a short and simple refrain after each verse or section of a verse.

Rubrics. Written directives (usually in red ink) for liturgical ceremonies.

Liturgical Glossary

Sacramentary. The book containing the various orations and other prayers used by the presiding priest during the liturgy.

Sequence. Originally a text added to the vocalization over the final vowel of the Alleluia to facilitate memorization of the melody. Today sequences (only four of them appear in the sacramentary) are optional except on Easter and Pentecost.

Synaxis (from the Greek for "meeting"). Any gathering of the people for worship; often applied to a gathering of the faithful for the liturgy.

Te Deum. A hymn of praise and thanksgiving dating from the early church and whose author is unknown.

Triduum. A three day celebration commemorating the passion, death, and resurrection of Christ; the triduum begins with the evening Mass of the Lord's Supper on Holy Thursday, reaches its climax with the Easter Vigil, and concludes with evening prayer on Easter Sunday.

Tune Meters. Letters or numbers (e.g., L.M. or 8.6.8.6) appearing in conjunction with a hymn text and indicating the number of lines in each verse and the number of syllables in each line.

Tune Names. Names assigned to hymn melodies as an easy means of identifying these melodies, e.g., "Moscow" or "St. Theodulph."

Vespers. From the latin *vesperae* ("evening"), this is the older name for what is now called evening prayer in the liturgy of the hours.